T0209948

AUTISM:

A Journey of Faith and Hope

AUTISM:
A Journey of Faith and Hope

Shannon Williams

authorHOUSE®

AuthorHouse™ LLC
1663 Liberty Drive
Bloomington, IN 47403
www.authorhouse.com
Phone: 1-800-839-8640

Published by AuthorHouse   09/28/2013

ISBN: 978-1-4918-1033-0 (sc)
ISBN: 978-1-4918-1034-7 (e)

Library of Congress Control Number: 2013914994

Cover Art by Andree F. Chambers

Any people depicted in stock imagery provided by Thinkstock are models, and such images are being used for illustrative purposes only. Certain stock imagery © Thinkstock.

This book is printed on acid-free paper.

DEDICATION

I dedicate this book to our beloved son Emmanuel
who is a precious gift from the Lord.
Thank God for your smile that lights up a room.
Thank God for your tenacious spirit!

I also dedicate this book to my loving husband, Derrick.
A man of faith and an awesome father! Thank God for
your love, unending support and your many sacrifices of
prayer and fasting!

Last but not least, I dedicate this book to all of the
children and families that are affected by the puzzling
neurological disorder called autism. May you gain faith for
today and hope for tomorrow!

Acknowledgements

I thank the Lord first and foremost. We would not have made it thus far without a sincere and heartfelt relationship with the Lord Jesus Christ! Thank you for your everlasting love and faithfulness!

I also thank our family members and friends. Thank you for your support and prayers! We love and appreciate you.

A special thank you to my mother Bernadine. Thank you for a providing unconditional love and support for me, my husband and my children. We love you mom!!

I also want to thank my late aunt Helen, who is now with Lord in Heaven. Aunt Helen encouraged and inspired me many, many years ago to write this book. I am eternally grateful for her many prayers, words of wisdom and love!

Contents

CHAPTER 1

A Journey Before
THE JOURNEY

Some children grow up with hopes and dreams of becoming a doctor, lawyer, teacher or a fire fighter. I dreamed of becoming a mother! As far as I can remember, I always wanted to be a mother. I remember being a young child and saying to my parents, "When I grow up I want to go to college, get married and have lots of children!" My father would always jokingly tease me. With a chuckle, he would say: "Oh I see, you will be a woman with a lot of degrees, sitting at home with a host of children!"

During my college career, God sent me a wonderful husband, who had the same passionate desire to have children. In fact, we often dreamed of being parents and we had many discussions about it. We tried and we tried to conceive a child for three consecutive years. The doctor said that we could not have children. In fact, he suggested that we see a fertility specialist. We decided that we would continue to trust the Lord for a miracle. After all, I reminded myself and my husband that "the just shall live by faith!" Hebrews 10:38

One day, a co-worker invited me to attend a Bible Study meeting at her church. It was an awesome Bible study . . . one like I had never seen or experienced! Every person in the church was actively involved in the Bible study! It was an exciting and engaging class. I thoroughly enjoyed myself. At the end of the class, the pastor asked the congregation if anyone desired prayer. My friend quickly stood up and said yes! She said: "Pastor, I invited my friend and her and her husband desire to have a baby. They have tried for quite some time." "Oh is that all," said the Pastor. He then beckoned me to walk to the altar. As I walked, I could feel the presence of God! When I reached the altar, the Pastor laid his hands on my forehead. He prayed the following prayer: "Lord, open this womb. Prepare this womb to carry a child, in Jesus Mighty Name." As the Pastor prayed I could feel a movement in my abdomen. Then the Lord spoke to me. God said: "I am performing a spiritual surgery on you, do not fear, only receive." I replied, "Yes, Lord!" This surgery went on for one hour! It was absolutely painless!

Nevertheless, I could feel the Lord moving things around in my abdomen! Glory to God!

About a month later my husband and I were preparing to attend Sunday Morning Worship service. I was getting ready and listening to a Christian radio program at the same time. It was Mother's Day. I was a bit sad because I was not yet a mother. I had just talked to the Lord about my sadness and about my desire to be a mother. After my brief talk with the Lord, I tuned into the Christian radio program again. The lady on the radio was preaching under the anointing of God. She stopped in the middle of her message. She said, "Wait a minute! There is a Woman of God listening to me right now. You are married to a Man of God, and he loves you very much. You have been trying to get pregnant for 3 years! The Lord says your time is here! Go out as an act of your faith and start purchasing baby clothes . . . because the baby is on its way!" My heart leaped. I immediately knew that she was talking to me. I cried and rejoiced at this awesome Word from the Lord. I quickly ran to share the good news with my husband, who was in the washroom.

The Bible tells us that faith without works is dead! James 2:20 Thus, as an act of faith my husband and I began to purchase baby clothes. About a month later we were pregnant! We were besides ourselves with joy, thankfulness and excitement! Our dream of being parents would be a complete reality in 9-10 months!

My pregnancy was basically uneventful for the first 4 months. I experienced no morning sickness and no unusual occurrences. One day after Sunday morning worship service I walked upstairs from the lower level of our home. Once I reached the top stair I was suddenly alarmed. My water bag had broken! I was home alone because my husband had gone to the grocery store. He returned shortly thereafter. I called my doctor and he said to meet him at the emergency room. By the time I had walked to the car the water bag had almost emptied itself.

Soon after arriving to the hospital, an ultra sound technician gave me an ultrasound. The doctor said that it did not look good. He said that we would miscarry our baby either that same week or the following week. I quickly told the doctor: "Not so. We are people of faith. God promised us this child. He is a boy child and the Lord told us to name him Emmanuel. We will have him at the God-appointed time!" The doctor quickly replied: "I am a doctor of faith. I will send you to a specialist."

I thank the Lord for the faith He gave us. He gave us a conquering, enduring and a victorious faith! Faith to believe Him and His promises over the report of man and over the existing circumstances! Faith to trust Him over what we felt, heard, and saw. Glory to God!

The very next day my husband took me to the specialist. The specialist took another ultrasound and he gave us a very gloomy report. He said that there was very little water left in the water bag. He also said that he was putting me on bed rest. He gave me specific instructions to stay in bed . . . . I could walk to the washroom and then immediately get back in bed. The specialist also stated that he was not going to put me in the hospital because at 4 months gestation the baby is not viable outside the mother. He also said that he doubted very seriously that our baby would survive this. But if the baby remained alive until the 6th month gestation he would hospitalize me. I quickly told him,

"The baby and I will make it to six months and beyond!" The doctor smiled and gave me a peculiar look.

Every week my husband took me to see the specialist. This was my only outing, as I heeded the doctor's orders regarding the strict bed rest. During one of our weekly trips to the specialist, I remember rolling down my car window on a cold frosty afternoon. My husband quickly said: "it's cold outside, what are you doing?" I chuckled and said: "Oh, I'm just enjoying some fresh outdoor air!" I was experiencing severe cabin fever!

During each weekly visit to the specialist, I was given an ultra sound to ensure that our baby was growing and thriving. The doctor affirmed that our child was a boy and that he was continuing to grow. At one point the doctor gave us a glimmer of hope. He told us that on rare occasions the water sac fills back up and seals itself. So my husband I began to fervently pray and specifically ask the Lord to refill the amniotic sac and seal it. We prayed and we prayed. My husband, a humble man of faith, fasted and prayed during the whole time that I was on bed rest. We prayed and we prayed. However, every time we went to the doctor the ultrasound displayed that there was less water in the bag than the previous week. We continued to pray and cry out to God about this matter. But each week, the doctors report was same . . . there is less water in the bag than the previous week. I was concerned and a bit confused. Thus, I humbly asked the Lord about it. I said, "Lord I don't understand why you haven't answered our prayer about refilling the water bag . . . we have prayed and prayed and we have maintained our faith." The Lord quickly responded to me. He said: "I am God. I don't need water in a bag to bring forth a healthy child. I am God all by myself." Upon hearing this, I cried and I cried. I sobbed and I wailed. I wholeheartedly repented because I realized that I had dictated to the Lord how to solve our dilemma. In fact I had boxed God in, by telling Him how I wanted Him to heal and fix our situation. What a terrible mistake. We cannot dictate to God how to heal and deliver. We must only trust Him and stand on the promises in His Holy Bible. Why? Because God is God and He alone is sovereign. No matter how things may look or seem, God is still in control. He has the final authority over our lives. We must only trust Him and believe what the Word of God (the Bible) tells us. We have to fight the good fight of faith. We must refuse to stagger at the promises of God (stated in the Holy Scriptures) through unbelief. We must fight to maintain our faith! We must be fully persuaded that what God has promised God is also able to perform! Romans 4:21. Hallelujah!

At the 6th month of pregnancy the doctor put me in a reputable hospital. I was monitored 24 hours a day by maternity nurses. This constant monitoring was critical to the health and livelihood of our unborn son. The amniotic fluid in the water bag helps to develop the baby's lungs. It also acts as a buffer to prevent the fetus from squeezing, grabbing, sitting on the umbilical cord. The umbilical cord is the unborn child's life line. Not only is it the conduit from which food travels from the mother to the child it also acts as a direct line to the baby's heart. Infants that grab on or sit on the cord can die because their heart rate will steadily decrease until the cord is released.

As I mentioned earlier, my husband prayed and fasted during the entire time I was on bed rest. The amazing thing is: I knew when he took a break from his fasting and praying. The enemy (Satan) would attack with fervency! I remember one time in particular. My husband decided to take a mini break from fasting. He did not inform me about his decision to break from fasting. That same day, I was suddenly awakened by the siren in my hospital room. A nurse quickly entered my room saying "mother, get up and move around, your baby has grabbed his umbilical cord and his heart rate is steadily decreasing!" I hurriedly obeyed her instructions and Emmanuel's heart rate began to climb and then stabilize. Thank God! Immediately thereafter, I telephoned my husband and said: "Honey, you must be off of your fast today." He paused and said, "Yes, but how did you know?" I explained to him about the incident that had taken place a few minutes earlier. Nevertheless, my husband resumed his fasting and praying immediately! The Bible tells us that this kind goeth not but by prayer and fasting! Matthew 17: 21. Prayer is definitely powerful, but fasting adds extra ammunition to our prayer!

During my long hospital stay the Lord sent me several hospital workers to encourage, minister to and to pray for. On a daily basis the maintenance workers, nurses, food service personnel, etc., would come to my room for prayer, scriptures and a word of encouragement. One of the hospital chaplains began to visit me on a regular basis for prayer and encouragement. She was so excited about how powerfully the Lord moved she started giving my hospital telephone number out (with my permission) to other patients that were in need of prayer and encouragement.

At one point I began to feel saddened and downcast. During this brief time of lowliness the enemy began to speak lies to my heart. He told me that nobody cared about me and that no one was praying for me. He said, "Here you are in the hospital and you are praying for all of these people . . . and no one is praying for you!" I accepted Satan's lies in my heart. I began to cry out to the Lord about how I was feeling. I told the Lord, "Lord here I am in the hospital and everyone is coming to me for prayer, and no one is praying for me!" The Lord quickly spoke to my heart: "This is not about you . . . this is about me and my work! You are in my hands." The Lord opened my eyes and he showed me how He had many people praying for me! I quickly dried my eyes and said "yes, Lord." I gained a new attitude and disposition. I joyfully began to encourage and pray for the hospital workers that God sent to my hospital room. It was refreshing to see how the Lord touched the lives of many people! Glory to God! The Lord had His perfect will and way!

The Lord taught my husband and I many valuable lessons during this time of testing and trial. He taught us how to totally trust Him and His Word, no matter how severe and discouraging a situation may look. We learned how to have conquering, persevering and enduring faith! He taught us how to cast down every imagination and thought that exalts itself against the knowledge of Christ. II Corinthians 10:5. Many times the doctors would enter my hospital room with negative reports. One time in particular, a doctor entered my room and said: "Please don't get your hopes up high. I doubt if your baby will live for a week after he is born. The patient down the hall was in a similar situation as you and her baby died 3 days after it was born." I heard the doctor's words but I did not receive his words in my heart. I immediately refused to accept them. I cast them down because they did not line up with God's Holy Word! I immediately spoke to my unborn son, Emmanuel— "Emmanuel you shall not die but live and declare the works of the Lord!" Psalm 118:17.

I had to continually put my total confidence and trust in the Lord. The Bible tells us that it is better to put your trust in the Lord than your confidence in man! Psalm 118:8. Each and every day I had to encourage myself in the Lord. In fact, I had encouraging and applicable Bible scriptures taped all over my hospital walls. I would read them, quote them, confess them several times a day. The Bible was literally my life source. It gave me life when I was surrounded by death. It sustained me and it protected me from the lies, tricks and snares of the devil. Although I was surrounded by the darkness of negative reports and words of despair and hopelessness, the Holy Scriptures literally became a lamp unto my feet and a light unto my path. Psalm 119:105. Hallelujah!

I spent a total of 96 days on bed rest—2 months at home and 1 ½ months in the hospital. My husband was a great encouragement to me as he continued to work, run the church, and visit me several times a week. Oh, how I appreciate his love and support, his prayers and his fasting! Words alone cannot express the gratefulness and love that I have for my husband! I also appreciate the support and prayers of my mother, siblings, aunts, grandparents, cousins, church members, and friends! I thank God for each person that prayed for me and my husband!

Our son Emmanuel arrived at the 7 1/2 month of gestation. He could comfortably fit in the palm of my hand, weighing 2 pounds 13 ounces. After the delivery of our son, a doctor came to speak to my husband and

I. The doctor said: "Your son will never be an Olympic Swimmer or a Marathon Runner . . . his lungs are under developed and he will always need a breathing machine." My husband and I did not accept the doctor's words. He was firmly standing on his medical knowledge and medical books . . . . but we were firmly standing on and holding fast to the Book of Books, which is The Word of God—The Holy Bible! It cannot fail! God promised us that His Word (the Holy Scriptures) will never return unto him void, but they would accomplish the very thing that he sent it out to do. Isaiah 55:11.

I visited the special care nursery when Emmanuel was three days old. When I arrived he was crying and hollering very loudly. As I began to look closer into his incubator I noticed that he was pulling his breathing tube out of his mouth. Utterly shocked and a bit dumfounded I watched him as he continued to scream and pull the breathing tube out of his mouth. The sirens over his incubator began to sound and the nurses came running. "Oh my God," said one nurse, "he has pulled his breathing tube out!" Another nurse yelled; "Give that baby some oxygen!" Meanwhile, Emmanuel continued to holler and scream! They quickly gave Emmanuel some oxygen and then telephoned a doctor to tell him about the occurrence. The doctor immediately ordered the nurses to take Emmanuel off of the oxygen. Emmanuel has been breathing on his own ever since! Glory to God!

Shortly thereafter, one doctor humbly told my husband and I, "We need more babies like Emmanuel, to humble us arrogant doctors!" He went on to say, "Your baby knows more than us doctors!" I quickly smiled and said: "No. God knows more . . . He's in charge!" The doctor smiled at my response. Soon thereafter, we received reports about the CEO of the hospital. The nurses told me that the CEO left his office to go to the Special Care Nursery to see Emmanuel—The miracle baby! Glory to God and God alone!!! Emmanuel stayed in the hospital for 4 weeks. He quickly gained weight and he grew stronger and stronger each day. God showed himself strong!

CHAPTER 2

THE JOURNEY BEGINS

My husband and I were absolutely overjoyed when the hospital released Emmanuel to come home. We were so very grateful to the Lord for our miracle baby, Emmanuel. There would be no more long trips to the hospital! Emmanuel gained weight and began to grow and grow! As an infant I noticed that he was sometimes difficult to calm. I also noticed that he was late reaching his developmental milestone for walking. He began to walk when he turned 18 ½months old. I spoke with a friend about her son who was also born pre-mature. She told me about the Early Intervention System. She said that they worked well with her son to help "catch him up with his peers." I decided to give them a call.

Several therapists came to our home to assess Emmanuel. They asked me and my husband a lot of questions. They also observed Emmanuel very closely. At one point several of the therapists began to whisper among themselves as they observed Emmanuel. I began to feel a bit uneasy and uncomfortable. I had no idea what they were talking about, but I had a "gut" feeling that it was not good. Shortly thereafter, they informed us that Emmanuel had sensory challenges and would need occupational therapy. They also said that his speech was delayed and that he could benefit from weekly speech therapy. Lastly, Emmanuel would need a developmental therapist to help improve his overall development. Nevertheless, each week involved several therapies for Emmanuel. I knew that preemies sometimes experience delays in their development. Thus, I wholeheartedly believed that the therapies would help Emmanuel "catch-up" with his peer group.

Emmanuel was an active little boy that loved peanut butter, popcorn, macaroni and cheese and fruit. Although he had limited language he loved to sing the tunes of his favorite television shows and quote his favorite scripture: "With God All things are possible!" Matthew 10:27b He also loved animals and he loved to look at books and to point to and name letters and numbers.

The time seemed to pass by rather quickly. It was time for Emmanuel to attend pre-kindergarten. The transition from the Early Intervention Program to pre-kindergarten was relatively smooth. My husband and I prayed for a God-fearing teacher that would work well with Emmanuel. The Lord answered our prayers! He sent us a God-fearing and Bible-believing teacher, teacher assistant and occupational therapist! The Lord is faithful! He hears and answers prayers.

As the school year progressed, Emmanuel's teacher had made several comments about Emmanuel indicating that she believed Emmanuel was on the autism spectrum. We resisted this thought adamantly! I began to research autism. I already knew Emmanuel had some sensory challenges. I also knew that every child with sensory challenges does not have autism . . . but that every child with autism has sensory challenges. Thus, I set out to build a case for our son and against autism. Our first IEP meeting was quickly approaching and I wanted to be prepared to "defend" Emmanuel.

As an early childhood educator of typically and atypically developing children, I had attended several IEP meetings before. Down through the years, I had heard the "backroom talk" and discussions about several children, prior to as well as after the IEP meetings. I had seen many parents sitting helpless and uninformed during IEP meetings. I was determined to be an educated and informed parent and an advocate for our son. I did not want our son to be labeled with Autism. I believed that when a child is labeled, sometimes, the teacher's expectations become low and halted. My husband and I had and still do have great expectations for our son!

I am also a firm believer that although some children learn differently than others, each child can learn. I also believe children will climb as high as their teacher's expectations allow. Somehow, labels seemed like glass ceilings. Glass ceilings are a bit deceptive, because while you look like you are advancing there is always a ceiling right above your head. This ceiling prevents you from advancing and excelling past a certain point. We certainly did not want that for Emmanuel! At any rate, my husband and I went to Emmanuel's IEP meeting equipped like soldiers prepared for battle. We had prayed to the Lord about the meeting. We had also requested the prayers of many family members and friends. The meeting began at the scheduled time. After everyone introduced themselves, I asked if I could say something. The case worker gave me permission to talk. I politely greeted everyone. I stated that while I respected each person and their profession, as Emmanuel's parents we were his first and primary teachers, and we knew Emmanuel better than any person sitting at that table. The room remained quite for a few seconds and they all agreed. The tone of the meeting seemed to change a little. The occupational therapist began to talk about her sessions with Emmanuel. The school psychologist also described his encounters with Emmanuel. He said that Emmanuel appeared to be on the Autism Spectrum. The Lord became our strength as the words Autism Spectrum seemed to pierce our hearts. I held back the tears and posed a question to the psychologist. I replied" I know Emmanuel has sensory challenges. I also know that all children with sensory challenges do not have autism. So where was the dividing line/deciding factor for our son Emmanuel?"

The school psychologist appeared to be a very kind fellow. However, he struggled with an answer. The occupational therapist came to his rescue. She said Mr. & Mrs. Williams I am so glad that we are on the same page as far as Emmanuel's sensory challenges. But to answer your question, the dividing line or the deciding factor would be lack of social skills and the language delays. I understood what she meant. However, I still resisted the idea of Emmanuel being labeled. I believe the main reason why I resisted the label is because we had faith in the Lord that Emmanuel would in fact "catch-up with his peers." But with each passing birthday we experienced a mixture of joy and sadness. Emmanuel turned three years old and he still wasn't talking like he should. Then he turned four years old and he still hadn't caught up. Each birthday was filled with a combination of joy and pain. Joy to have our son. Joy to see our son physically grow and reach another birthday. But also tears and indescribable pain. Another year had come and gone and our dear son had not "caught up." To compound our inner hurt and pain, we've had to endure the stares and comments of others. People would stare at Emmanuel when he was loud, overactive or having a meltdown. We have had our share of hurtful stares, whispers and audible comments . . . both in and out of the church. One person suggested that all Emmanuel needed was a "good but whipping!" While another person jokingly called Emmanuel a wild child. Countless incidents have occurred in public places, the church and at family gatherings. One our teen-aged neighbors joking mocked the way Emmanuel communicated and flapped his hands. He did this as my husband walked in our driveway. One of the young man's friends quickly told him that he was wrong, but still participated in the mocking and laughing.

Although we have experienced many hurts and disappointments, God has graced us in such awesome ways. He has used our experiences to build character, compassion, love, longsuffering, understanding and forgiveness in our hearts. We thank God for giving us a heart and a mind to forgive those that trespass against us. Just as the Lord forgives us when we trespass against Him and other people! Thank God for his grace and mercy! The Lord is teaching us how to apply the scripture which says: "great peace have those that love thy law, and nothing shall offend them." Psalm 119: 165. We are understanding and learning this lesson daily.

CHAPTER 3

THE DIAGNOSIS

Emmanuel was now four years old. He could speak many words, but he rarely spoke in phrases or sentences. One day, my husband took Emmanuel to visit his pediatrician. Emmanuel suffered from a series of ear infections and colds. This particular day, Emmanuel had a huge meltdown in the doctor's office. For those that may not know, meltdowns are like huge tantrums. They can consist of loud crying, screaming, falling out on the floor, head banging, other self-destructive behaviors, etc. For the most part, meltdowns are very difficult to control and they last for a varied amount of time. Children that are in the beginning and or middle of a meltdown are usually difficult to calm. It takes a lot of prayer, patience and time.

During this time, the main goal is to keep the child safe and to calm the child down.

Meltdowns can be triggered by an illness, new and unfamiliar environments, sights, sounds, odors, etc. At any rate, my husband later described this meltdown with tears in his eyes and pain in his heart. His heartfelt description made me cry out to the Lord with a heart filled with grief. My cry was a word less cry. A cry that could only be interpreted by God.

Having witnessed this painful episode, the doctor told my husband that she wanted to speak with both of us about Emmanuel. Thus, a few days later we came in for a sit down with Emmanuel's pediatrician. She closed her office door and told us that after witnessing Emmanuel's meltdown, she became very concerned about Emmanuel. She was also concerned about us, as Emmanuel's parents. She wanted to know how often Emmanuel had meltdowns and also if we had a support system to help us. Our support system was very small and limited and Emmanuel's tantrums were increasing in occurrence and in duration. With a gentleness and a concerned heart, Emmanuel's pediatrician recommended that we take Emmanuel to see a neurologist. She gave us the name and telephone number of a local child neurologist. We called the neurologist and scheduled an appointment. About a month prior to the scheduled appointment I began to feel a little uneasy. I went to the Lord and I told him all about my feelings of insecurity. I began to reflect on all of the prophecies that we had received about Emmanuel prior to his birth and thereafter. So many awe inspiring words about the great call that God has on Emmanuel's life! One powerful preacher told us that Emmanuel was going to travel to the nations to preach the Word of God! Glory to God! In my personal, private prayer time I said: "Lord, we have received so many prophetic words regarding Emmanuel's destiny and call. But this time, I need to hear directly from you regarding Emmanuel. Lord, please speak directly from your mouth to my ear." This simple prayer enabled me to cast my cares upon the Lord. Amazingly, I was strengthened and encouraged!

About three weeks later the Lord answered my prayer. One morning about 3 am I was up praying. During this prayer time, I was praying for many people and many circumstances. In fact, I had forgotten about my own prayer concerning Emmanuel.

As I lied down on my bed the Lord allowed me to "hear" into the future. For 15 minutes the Lord allowed me to hear a future sermon preached by Emmanuel ! Yes!!! The Lord allowed me to "hear" into the future! Emmanuel spoke with an adult voice and his sermon was one of faith and encouragement. He spoke very eloquently, admonishing the audience to never give up on their children and on their hopes and dreams. He said: "we walk by faith and not by sight! Stand and believe God no matter how things may look or seem. God is higher than the reports of man!"

He then went on to tell of his own testimony and how his parents completely trusted God for his healing! "My parents refused to give up on God or me . . . and look at me now! I am completely healed!" I also heard the audience as they cheered and praised the Lord fervently with cries of joy and excitement and handclaps.

This was an awesome and life changing experience! I cannot begin to describe the joy, assurance and excitement that I felt as I listened to Emmanuel speak. I was fully awake during this entire time and I immediately began to cry, thank and worship the Lord! The Lord, our God is good and worthy to be praised! I am still rejoicing in the goodness and faithfulness of our God! I shared the details about this incident with my husband. He was equally excited and thankful!

Our appointment with the child neurologist was about a week away. My husband's fervent and effectual prayer was that we would receive a good report from the neurologist. I gently explained that whatever the neurologist's report was, my faith was still in God, who has the final authority over Emmanuel's life. God's report, and God's promises always transcend the reports of men. After a brief discussion about the matter, my husband said he understood, but that he was still trusting God for a good report.

We arrived to the neurologist's office in a timely fashion. It was a cold and uninviting place. From the moment you entered the office lobby you were bombarded with less than hospitable signs about NO EATING or DRINKING, etc. Except for the signs, the walls were grey and bare . . . no children's posters, paintings, or books. Furthermore, the wait time was extremely long. We waited one and half hours just to go back to the examining room. We had to break the rules and feed our son, as we were not forewarned about the long wait times. The front desk attendant seemed preoccupied. She offered no sympathy or explanation about the long wait time. She quickly escorted us to the examining room. There, we had to wait an additional 30 minutes to see the doctor. By this time, Emmanuel was very restless and very active. The doctor briefly introduced herself and immediately began to ask us a lot of questions. She observed Emmanuel very closely. The examination and questioning lasted for an hour. Then came the verdict. She diagnosed Emmanuel with Autism. As the tears began to fill our eyes, the neurologist seemed not to notice and she continued to talk. No attention was given to our pain and grief. No compassion was shown. No recommendations were given for sources of future help or support. In fact, we did not receive any additional information. The neurologist only suggested that we take Emmanuel to get a blood test and then schedule a follow-up appointment.

The visit to see the neurologist had been 3 hours long and emotionally draining! We were both mentally and physically tired and the ride home seemed to take forever. My husband and I were both stunned and saddened by the diagnosis. However, at this particular time, I seemed to have a little more strength and faith. Married couples seemed to "balance one another." In some instances one spouse maybe stronger than the other and vice versa. God knows how to pair his people together in a complimentary fashion. At any rate, being a bit stronger, in this instance, I desperately tried to encourage my husband with words of faith and with scriptures. My words seemed to hit a brick wall. My husband was so overcome with grief he could not receive my words of encouragement. My attempts to lift his spirit were seemingly unsuccessful. He cried and cried. When we arrived home, my husband immediately climbed in bed. His body was in a fetal position and cried himself to sleep. It was about 5 pm, and he did not awaken until the next morning. Seeing him in that condition increased my pain greatly. Thus, I began to cry out to God in prayer. I asked God for strength wisdom and direction. I asked the Lord for faith to overcome this test and trial. Lastly, as an act of faith, I thanked God for Emmanuel's complete healing and deliverance.

The next morning my husband got up early. He mentally debated on whether he should go to work, as he still felt very sad and emotionally drained. He decided to go to work anyway. When he arrived to work, one of his co-workers anxiously approached him. He looked at my husband and said: "Can you tell what it means to count your blessings?" My husband response was: "huh?" The co-worker repeated the question: "Can you tell me what it means to count your blessings?" "Yes," my husband responded. "To count your blessings means to reflect on all that the Lord has already done for you and to be thankful, no matter what test, trial or difficulty that you might currently be faced with." The co-worker smiled, said "thank you" and he walked away. God is awesome! It amazes me when I think about how wonderfully the Lord orchestrated this ordeal! God used the simple question of a co-worker to shed His eternal light on our dark and gloomy situation! Hallelujah! Glory to God!!

A few hours later, a lady approached my husband while he was working. She said: "Sir, are you the reverend?" My husband hesitated briefly and said "well, yes I am a reverend." She said "good! I was looking for you yesterday, but your co-workers said you were not working." My husband was a bit shocked, because he had never seen or met this lady before. The lady went on to say: "Reverend, I just wanted to tell you that God is good! And God is a healer!" She went on to describe in full detail her testimony of a miracle healing. My husband listened intently and was greatly encouraged! The Lord is truly amazing!! He is very mindful and concerned about his children! He sent a total stranger, perhaps an angel, to encourage my husband. This reminds me of the scripture that says: "Be not forgetful to entertain strangers: for thereby some have entertained angels unawares." Hebrews 13:2.

I wholeheartedly rejoiced when I received the telephone call from my husband describing these miraculous occurrences! I was both strengthened and encouraged! Praise the Lord! As I rejoiced, I began to reflect on Emmanuel's name. It means "God with us." Matthew 1: 23. Glory to God! God is with us! And if God be with us he is certainly for us! If God is for you he is more than the world against you. And at times autism and its challenges can seem bigger than the world! But God! God has all power in His hands! Our life and our times are in His hands. Hope in God! Psalm 42:11.

No matter what the test or trial that you may be enduring . . . God is still in control and He has the final authority over our lives! Tests and trials are meant to strengthen us by drawing us closer to the Lord. They are meant to build character and endurance in us. Jesus experienced the ultimate suffering for mankind. And as followers of Jesus we will also have to endure suffering. He said: If you suffer with Christ, you will also reign with Christ!" 2 Timothy 2: 12. Think about this . . . the Lord never promised us a bed of roses. If he had promised us a bed of roses, there would still be thorns! The Lord did however promise us so many wonderful promises. He promised to be with us until the end. He said that He would never leave us or forsake us! Hebrews 13:5. He also promised that we were more than conquerors because He loves us! Romans 8:37 He promised to be a very present help in the time of trouble! Psalm 46:1. God is not like man. Man may promise something but may not fulfill the promises for one reason or another. But what God has promised, He is faithful to fulfill! All of his promises are yea (which means yes) and amen (it is so)! 2 Corinthians 1:20. God said that His Word (His promises) would never return to him void, but it would accomplish the very thing that he sent it out to do! Isaiah 55:11 Hallelujah!

God made Abraham a promise. He promised Abraham that he would be the father of many nations. Genesis 17:4. Abraham had to walk by faith because his wife was barren and also well beyond child bearing age. The odds were stacked against Him. The situation looked bleak and hopeless. But the Bible tells us that Abraham staggered not at the promises of God through unbelief. But he was strong in faith. He was fully persuaded that what God had promised, God was also able to perform! Romans 4: 20-21. Take a moment to think about this. Abraham staggered not at the promise of God through unbelief! When I think about a person staggering, I immediately envision an intoxicated person trying to walk. Intoxication often causes a person's footing and balance to be unsure. It can make a person stagger. Similarly, we stagger at the promises of God when we become intoxicated with our trials and tribulations. We literally become overly focused on what we see, hear, feel and smell . . . and we enter a drunken-like spiritual state. Drunkenness impairs a person's mental faculties, their speech and their physical capabilities. Thus, as we began to stagger, our speech begins to reflect doubt instead of faith and our minds begin to succumb to thoughts of defeat and hopelessness. And then, last but not least, our walk with the Lord is adversely affected. Our walk of faith is somehow halted as we get stuck in a quick sand of doubt, discouragement and unbelief. I strongly encourage you . . . . no matter how difficult the trial or test, make a determination in your heart and mind to stagger not! Ask the Lord to help you become fully persuaded, fully assured, fully fixed, fully convinced that *God will* deliver, *God will* heal, *God will* strengthen and *God will* provide! Settle your mind and heart today. It is no longer a question of *will God?* Instead it is a statement of faith and a faith-filled declaration: GOD WILL! Hallelujah! God is faithful! Be strong in the Lord and in the power of His might! Ephesians 6:10. David said he would of fainted unless he had believed to see the goodness of the Lord in the land of the living! Psalm 27:13. Refuse to faint! Resist the temptation to give in and to give up! Believe to see the goodness of the Lord while you are yet alive! Those that do not know God often say I have to see "it" in order to believe "it". To them seeing is believing. However, to the born-again Christian, belief is the prerequisite to seeing the complete manifestation of the belief. In other words, Christians believe first and then see the fruit of their faith and belief! Glory to God!!

In the very next verse, David gives some sound and wise instruction. "Wait on the Lord: be of good courage, and he shall strengthen thine heart: wait I say, on the Lord." Psalm 27: 14. David fully knew what it meant to wait on the Lord. He was anointed to be King at age 16 but did not reign as King until he was 30 years old. During the interim time he was chased in the wilderness by a jealous and unrighteous King named Saul. Furthermore, after David was crowned King, his rebellious son, Absalom, chased David, in an attempt to take his life.

Waiting on the Lord rests upon a wholehearted decision to trust and joyfully serve God in spite of difficult tests and trials. Those that wait on the Lord must wait with an attitude of gratitude and thankfulness. Thankfulness and gratitude naturally occur when we meditate on God's Word instead of the disturbing situation that we are currently facing. God's Word is filled with words of life and encouragement! Another thing that's breeds a heart of thankfulness is reflecting on what God has already done in our lives as well as the lives of our love ones and friends. As we focus our hearts and minds on God's Holy Word and on past testimonies we receive supernatural strength. An overcoming strength! The joy of the Lord is our strength! Nehemiah 8: 10. Little joy, little strength! Big joy, Big strength!

We must continually guard our hearts against temptations to murmur and complain. We must refuse to fall into a "pity party." Although the Lord had been faithful to the children of Israel, they still maintained an attitude of ungratefulness, and complaining during their

CHAPTER 4

The Just Shall Live By Faith

What is faith? Faith is a wholehearted belief in God and His supremacy. It's knowing, without a shadow of a doubt that God has the final authority over our lives. It is believing that God's word (the Holy Bible) is true and it is the standard for everyday living. Faith is always knowing that God is ruling, reigning and in control!

"Now faith is the substance of things hoped for, the evidence of things not seen." Hebrews 11:1. It is very important to note that the scripture says "now faith." We need faith for the situations and circumstances that we are faced with at this very present time. We need faith for right now. Faith to deal with current heartaches and pains.

Faith to keep on keeping on. Faith to stand in the midst of adversity!

The Bible says that "the just shall live by faith." Hebrews 10:28. As I take time to meditate on the above scripture tears fill my eyes. I am reflecting on how faith has carried me through many of my darkest and difficult days. I shutter when I think about what my life would be like without faith. Surely, it would not be a life worth living. I imagine that a faithless life would be a hopeless life.

We need faith to face daily tests, trials and struggles. We need faith for daily survival. We need faith to maintain a healthy mental and emotional state of being. We need faith to shield us from every fiery dart of the devil! Ephesians 6:16. In Romans 1:17 God said: "The just shall live by faith." The just are those that have been redeemed and made righteous by the blood of Jesus. I am talking about the blood brought Christians, the born-again believers. The phrase "shall live" is very, very important. Naturally speaking, our bodies need several things to thrive and function. Some of these things include food, water, and oxygen. Our bodies can function without food for a big length of time and without water for a short period of time. Our bodies can also function if certain organs shut down. However, our bodies cannot function or live if our hearts stop beating. Faith to a Christian is like a heartbeat to a body. When the heart fails and stops beating death typically follows. When a Christian loses faith their spiritual life also begins to fail and die.

Take a moment and consider the function of a heart. The heart is a muscle. Its main job is to transport blood around our bodies. The blood supplies our bodies with the oxygen and nutrients it needs. It also carries away waste. The Bible tells us that the life of the flesh is in the blood. Leviticus 17: 1. Thus, our blood provides life to our bodies. Just as the heart is a muscle, our faith is like a muscle. The more we exercise our faith, the stronger our faith becomes. Our continued, enduring and unrelenting faith causes "life" to be diffused in our daily affairs, challenges, etc. That same faith causes the waste—the dead and unfruitful thoughts, attitudes, circumstance, etc., to be forcefully removed from our lives!

The just shall live by faith! Romans 1:17. Christians survive, thrive, maintain their mental posture, and overcome adversity, through and by their faith in God! Faith is belief and total trust in God. The Bible tells us that "now faith is the substance of things hoped for and the evidence of things not seen." Hebrews 11:1. We need faith for right now—this very moment in our lives! It is important to note that faith is made up of what we are hoping for. We need not hope for what we already have. We hope for those things that we do not already possess. Thus, faith is evidenced or proven by things we cannot see with our natural eyes.

It is very easy to get discouraged, distressed, perplexed overwhelmed and burdened by what we see with our natural eyes. The devil works in the present time and overtime to attack our faith. However, I encourage to you change your focus, adjust your lenses and look through the eyes of faith. The Bible tells us not to focus on the things which are seen. Instead, we are to focus on the things which are not seen (God, and his heavenly host of angels moving on our very behalf, etc). Why? Because the things which are seen are temporary; but the things which are not seen are eternal. 2Corinthians 4:18. Glory to God!

The Bible also tells us to "cast down imaginations and every high thing that exalteth itself against the knowledge of God and to bring into captivity every thought to the obedience of Christ." 2 Corinthians 10: 5. The phrase "cast down" means to violently and authoritatively throw something down. Imaginations and every high thing include thoughts, ideas, advice, opinions, comments, fears, etc. Thus, we must take authority in the name of Jesus and violently cast down and throw away every thought, idea, etc., that tries to exalt itself against the knowledge of Christ! The knowledge of Christ is the knowledge of the Bible. For the Bible tells us: "In the beginning was the Word (Bible) and the Word was with God and the Word was God. "John 1:1. Then thirteen verses after that the verse reads: "And the Word was made flesh, and dwelt among us, and we beheld his Glory, the Glory as the only begotten of the Father, full of grace and truth." John 1:14.

The knowledge of Christ includes every promise that God gives us in his Holy Word. It includes every command, and every word of instruction and encouragement! We must continually cast down every thought, word of advice, comments, etc., that opposes the Word of God!

The last portion of 2 Corinthians 10:5 tells us to "bring into captivity every thought to the obedience of Christ." It takes wisdom, knowledge and strength to capture something. Wisdom involves fully understanding your position as a child of the Lord. As a child of the King, you have certain rights and privileges as well as God-given authority. You have power, in the Name of Jesus to take authority and cast down the works of Satan! God has given you power to overcome the devil and all of his plans, schemes and traps! Take your position as a victor and not a victim. Knowledge, on the other hand, involves knowing with your mind and heart, the promises that God has given us in His Holy Word. One promise that comes to mind: "Beloved, I wish above all things that you would prosper, and be in health, even as your soul prospers! 3 John 1:2. The Lord wants us to prosper spiritually, physically, mentally, and emotionally! Glory to God!

I must add that the Word of God is our manual. It is the road map of how we are to travel a victorious journey on the road of Christian life. It is a "lamp unto our feet and light unto our path." Psalm 119: 105. It will lead us through every dark and gloomy situation. It will guide us through times of confusion. It will order our steps when we are not sure which way to turn!

Let's revisit the latter portion of 2 Corinthians 10:5. It requires strength to bring something into captivity. One must exert more strength than the thing that's being captured. Where does one get this strength in midst of storms and hard struggles? The Bible tells us that the joy of the Lord is our strength. Nehemiah 8:10. Sometimes we have to ask the Lord to give us a praise song to sing. Singing scripturally based songs and praising the Lord while enduring hard tests and trial brings joy to our own hearts and also the heart of the Lord. As we praise God, we miraculously begin to reflect on the goodness of God . . . and all that he has already done in our lives. The Bible tells us that "we overcome the devil by the blood of the lamb and the word of our testimony." Revelation 12:1. The blood of Jesus redeems us, sets us free, protects, and heals us! Reflecting on past testimonies encourages and strengthens us. Testimonies remind us that God is ALL powerful, ALL knowing and FOREVER faithful! Testimonies remind us that "with God nothing is impossible!" Luke 1:37.

CHAPTER 5

Enduring Hardness

I am very familiar with enduring hardness. I believe that I have cried enough tears to fill Lake Michigan. I have cried both publicly and privately about our son. I have sobbed and wept during the midnight hour and during daybreak. At times, I have literally felt like my very heart was being stabbed, punctured and ripped apart. I have felt frustrated and overwhelmed. Oh, the pain has been tremendous and at times, unbearable. But the Lord has made His children a very special promise in Matthew 11:28-30. "Come unto me, all ye that labor and are heavy laden, and I will give you rest. Take my yoke upon you, and learn of me; for I am meek and lowly in heart: and ye shall find rest unto your souls. For my yoke is easy, and my burden is light." I often reflect on this scripture during the most difficult and troubling times. I have also talked to the Lord about this. God knows all things and He always has our best interest at hand. The scriptures tell us that God loves us and is so concerned about us that he keeps the very tears that we shed. Psalm 56:8. I sometimes chuckle and think I must have my very own river of tears in Heaven!

As I think about my pain I am reminded about my co-workers. They often call me "smiley." Many say that I come to work everyday with a smile and that I am always cheerful and kind. Sometimes they tell me that I look well rested. I thank God that I am still able to walk in joy and peace from day to day. I also appreciate the well-meaning comments of my co-workers. However, one never knows what a person may be enduring every day in their home and private life. Sometimes, there is a notable story behind a person's laugh and smile. There is definitely a story behind my daily smiles. A story that is seeped in pain and sufferings yet rooted and grounded in faith and hope. The kind of faith and hope that knows a brighter day is coming. The kind of faith that refuses to give in or give up. The kind of faith that latches on to the promises of God and refuses to let go! The Bible promises us that "weeping may endure for a night but joy comes in the morning!" Psalm 30:5.

Behind my daily smile is my brokenness and an enduring faith in the Lord. Many days I would arrive to work with less than 3-4 hours of sleep. Sometimes Emmanuel would get sick or become unexplainably fretful. He couldn't verbalize his feelings to me or my husband. I have cried many times because he could not tell me what was hurting and what was wrong. He would just whine, cry and have tantrums all during the evening and night. In addition to crying, I would pray and ask the Lord for guidance and direction. The Lord is faithful! He would give me and or my husband insight regarding what was wrong with Emmanuel.

Many other times I would suffer from mental as well as physical exhaustion. Exhausted from dealing with day to day issues like the repeated clean-ups that must be done as Emmanuel liked to throw everything on the floor. Additionally, Emmanuel is very active and curious and he requires a lot of constant supervision. He likes to put non-edible items in his mouth and he is also very, very mischievous!

Other daily challenges include family vacation, trips to the grocery store, rides in the car, getting ready for school, etc. Sometimes people take the simple things in life for granted. Simple things like taking a trip to the local grocery store or a walk around your neighborhood. These "simple" things can become very complicated and stressful when having to care for and raise a child that has disabilities or challenges. Although disabilities differ in severity they all include their own set of challenges. Autism can be very demanding, and puzzling. Sometimes the behaviors are very violent, sudden and unexplainable. The meltdowns and tantrums can occur at any time and in any place. They can also last for varied amounts of time.

The Bible tells us "to endure hardness like a good soldier of Jesus Christ." 2 Timothy 2:3. Good soldiers have a determination in their hearts to fight and never give up. In fact, they will fight until victory or death. Similarly, Christians are to fight the good fight of faith and never give up. We are to fight until we take our last breath.

Moreover, good soldiers fight . . . . even when they are wounded and hurting. They fight when they face fearful and frightening situations. They fight when they are tired and weary. Good soldiers endure hardness and refuse to buckle under pressing and disturbing situations. Good soldiers fight until they see victory or death. The Bible tells us to "fight the good fight of faith." 1 Timothy 6:12. It is indeed a good fight because it is a fixed fight. It is fixed fight because as long as we maintain our faith, walk in obedience to the lord and remain fully connected to Him, we win!!

As Christians, we are soldiers in the army of Jesus Christ. Our battles are not flesh and blood battles. Our battles are spiritual battles. Ephesians 6:12. Thus, we have to fight the good fight of faith even during the most difficult situations. We have to fight when we are wounded from the rigors of daily living and from the attacks of the enemy. We have to fight when we are faced with fearful situations and circumstances. We have to fight when we are feeling tired and weary in our minds and our bodies.

As a young child I never liked to fight. I had cousins however, that loved to fight. They picked fights and won. I, on the other hand, would avoid fights at all costs. I was bullied often and I eventually learned how to defend myself. But, I still preferred not to fight. As a Christian, however, I had to learn how to fight. Fighting is a daily part of the Christian's life. Christians constantly have to fight against the powers of darkness, against the temptations of the enemy and the schemes and tricks of the devil. The Bible tells us that "we wrestle not against flesh and blood but against powers and the rulers of darkness in high places." Ephesians 6:12. The term wrestle means a close hand to hand, body to body fight. Thus, our fight with the enemy is a close in proximity fight, whereby the enemy is always lurking near seeking to devour the people of God. His goal is to devour us mentally, spiritually, emotionally, and physically. But thank God because "we are more than conquerors because Jesus loves us (and we follow Him)." Romans 8:37. We are more than overcomers! "Ye are of God, little children, and have overcome them: because greater is he that is in you, than he that is in the world." 1 John 4:4. Furthermore, the Lord is our shield, our buckler, our protector, our mind regulator, our strength, our refuge and our fortress!

Satan works overtime to attack our faith in God. Christians have to fight to maintain their faith in the

Lord. This fight is a spiritual fight and not a carnal fight. The Bible tells us that "the weapons of our warfare are not carnal, but mighty through God to the pulling down of strongholds." 2 Corinthians 10: 4. Thus, we have to fight with the spiritual weapons that God has given us. These weapons include utilizing the name of Jesus, prayer, fasting, faith, the blood of Jesus, and the Word of God.

"The name of Jesus is a strong tower. The righteous run to it and are safe." Proverbs 18:10. Satan hates the name of Jesus. But Jesus has given us permission, power and authority to use his name when we pray. In fact, we are to pray in the name of Jesus. And when we pray we are to believe that God hears and answers our prayers. The scriptures tell us that "those that come to God must believe that He is God and that he is a rewarder of those that diligently seek him." Hebrews 11:6. Our belief that God is indeed God (he is sovereign) is the core foundation of our faith. God rewards those that diligently and consistently seek him.

Prayer is communication with God. It involves speaking to the Lord and listening to the Lord. Prayer should be done formally—whereby you have a regularly scheduled daily prayer time and informally whereby you talk with the Lord while you are driving your car, doing household chores, and all throughout your day. I have learned first hand that many things in life are too difficult to carry and bear. Thus, taking time to talk with the Lord is essential to our spiritual well being. We must daily cast all of our cares (burdens and concerns) upon the Lord because he cares for us. 1 Peter 5: 7. This casting takes place in an intimate prayer time.

There are some things that are only resolved through prayer and fasting. When the disciples could not cast the devil out of the boy with a lunatic (epileptic) spirit, they asked Jesus the reason for their lack of success. Jesus told them they had little faith and he also added: "this kind goeth not but by prayer and fasting." Mark 9:29. Prayer is a powerful weapon against the enemy. But when coupled with fasting . . . . the power is increased expeditiously! Fasting buffers one's own flesh thereby giving complete reign to the Spirit of God. It does not twist the arm of God to perform a certain request. Prayer and fasting shows the Lord your heart and commitment toward Him and the situation that you may be facing.

The blood of Jesus is another powerful weapon that we have against the attacks and snares of the devil. The Bible tells us that "we overcome the devil by the blood of the lamb . . ." Revelations 12:1. The Lamb is Jesus. "Behold the lamb of God which taketh away the sins of the world." John 1:29. Jesus blood is so very powerful. It is the only thing that can wash away sin. Satan hates the blood of Jesus because it washes away the sins of mankind. The Bible tells us "without the shedding of blood there is no remission of sin." Hebrews 9:22. Thus, Jesus blood redeems us, and protects from the plans of the enemy. In the Old Testament, Pharaoh ordered the 1st born of the

Hebrews to be killed. God told Moses to apply the blood of an unblemished lamb upon the doorposts of all the Hebrew people and the death Angel would pass over the homes of the Hebrew people. Exodus Chapter 12. Today, Jesus is our unblemished lamb. He knew no sin, and his blood is free from sin. Similarly, we can apply the precious blood of Jesus (through our prayer) to our homes, various situations, children and the devil cannot touch us. Satan flees from the blood of Jesus!

Faith is another weapon that the Christian soldier must have. Faith, according to the Word of God, is a shield that protects against the fiery darts of the devil. Ephesians 6: 16. The shield of faith quenches all of the fiery darts of the wicked one. Many of the tests and trials that Christians experience are indeed fiery and difficult. But faith in God and his infinite wisdom acts as a shield that literally protects us from the fiery darts of the devil. Our shield of faith puts the devil's fires out. Satan's fiery darts include lies, discouragement, weariness, fear, hopelessness and despair. When we stand in faith the devil's arsenal of weapons is made null and void. When we struggle with maintaining our faith we are no longer shielded from the attacks of the devil. The fiery darts of the enemy wound us. Wounds and injuries greatly hinder us while we are yet in the battle. Thus, the enemy gains the opportunity to have the upper hand. We must fight to maintain our faith at all times. And it is indeed a fight! The devil works overtime to get us to drop our shield of faith through weariness, double-mindedness, depression, discouragement, oppression, etc. We must fight to maintain our faith! We must purposefully refocus our thoughts and our minds on the goodness and faithfulness of God. This can be achieved by spending time praising and worshipping God—in spite of our troubles and difficulties. It can also be achieved listening to faith building messages and sermons. The Bible tells us that "faith comes by hearing and hearing by the Word of God." Romans 10:17. Maintaining our faith keeps our shield of faith ready at all times, thereby protecting us from the tricks and traps of the devil!

God gives us one offensive weapon to use against the enemy . . . the sword of the spirit. This sword is the Word of God. It is powerful and sharper than any 2-edged sword. Ephesians 6:17. We can read the Word of God, study the Word of God and hide the Word of God in our hearts. It is our rule of conduct and faith. It gives us all of the promises of God. It leads and guides us in our daily affairs. It is a weapon against the enemy . . . God said his words are spirit and they are life. John 6:63. Thus, when we apply the Word of God to our struggles, difficulties, etc., we are literally applying life, vigor and power. The devil, on the other hand, applies death and hopelessness and God applies life and hope! Additionally, the Word of God is a lamp unto our feet and a light unto our path. During our most dark, dreary and confusing times, the

Word of God will bring light and clarity unto our pathway and our various situations.

We can hold God's Word above what we see and hear. We can hold God's Word above the reports of men. God said His word will never return unto Him void (empty) but it will accomplish the very thing that He sent it out to do. Isaiah 55:11. Thus, when we apply the Word of God to our lives, we are literally focusing on and holding fast to what God's Word says versus what we see, feel and hear. We literally hold on to life (God and His promises) and steadfastly refuse what Satan tries to present to us every day (death, defeat and hopelessness). We began to speak what God's Word says pertaining to our situation instead of what we feel or have heard.

CHAPTER 6

The 4 Hour Cry

One summer, we took a road trip to Kentucky to visit my brother and his family. At that time, they had a couple of horses. Our son Emmanuel loves animals, especially dogs and horses! Thus, I was very excited about the idea of Emmanuel being able to see and pet a horse! As I took Emmanuel to see the horses, he showed a bit of resistance. Then he quickly covered his eyes with his hands. Initially, I could not understand his behavior . . . . then suddenly I understood. The horses had flies all over their eyes. Emmanuel does not like flies. Emmanuel tightly shielded his eyes with his hands. I quickly led him away from the horses. We walked back into my brother and sister-in law's house.

We returned home several days later. Emmanuel woke up in the middle of the night with a very loud scream and cry. He had both of his hands tightly covering his eyes. He was petrified! We tried to calm him and console him, but we were very unsuccessful. From the way he kept his hands over his eyes, we surmised that he had a nightmare about the horses and the flies. His loud, screeching cry lasted for a total of four hours! We tried everything from giving him juice and food, to rocking him to calm him down, to massaging him, but he only seemed to get louder. We sobbed and cried with him and for him. Our hearts seemed to break into a million tiny pieces because Emmanuel couldn't communicate with us and we were unable to communicate with him. It was a very emotional time. The enemy tried to make us feel hopeless, powerless and defeated. He succeeded for a while. We spent about 3 hours trying to solve this situation with natural means. Suddenly we realized that nothing was working. We had to fight to take our attention off of the luminous situation and put it on the Lord. God and God alone could provide us with a solution to this heart wrenching and disturbing situation. The Bible says that "the Lord is a very present help in the time of trouble." Psalm 46: 1. The Word of God also says that "the righteous cry and the Lord delivers them out of all their troubles." Psalm 34: 17. After three hours of painful cries and agony, we were more than desperate for a solution. Out of sheer pain and desperation, my husband cried out to the Lord. The Lord led my husband to put his hand on Emmanuel's forehead and pray. I quickly joined in. We prayed for God's peace to fall upon Emmanuel. We prayed in our natural language and in our heavenly language. Emmanuel's cries began to decrease in intensity and volume. He began to slowly calm down. I know that it may sound a bit strange . . . . but is was through this particular test, that we learned to use prayer as our first arm of defense. Remember, when you uncertain about what to do, PRAY. When you are void of full understanding, PRAY. When the enemy comes in like a flood . . . . PRAY. When your emotions are a wreck and going haywire . . . . PRAY. Pray in faith and pray with faith. Pray expecting an immediate answer.

Chapter 7

Trust

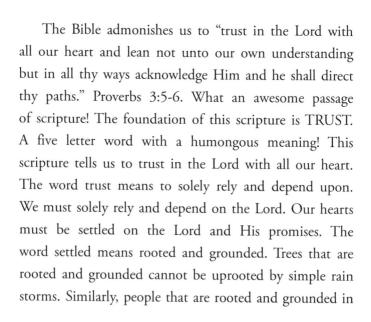

The Bible admonishes us to "trust in the Lord with all our heart and lean not unto our own understanding but in all thy ways acknowledge Him and he shall direct thy paths." Proverbs 3:5-6. What an awesome passage of scripture! The foundation of this scripture is TRUST. A five letter word with a humongous meaning! This scripture tells us to trust in the Lord with all our heart. The word trust means to solely rely and depend upon. We must solely rely and depend on the Lord. Our hearts must be settled on the Lord and His promises. The word settled means rooted and grounded. Trees that are rooted and grounded cannot be uprooted by simple rain storms. Similarly, people that are rooted and grounded in the Word of God will not be uprooted by the storms of life. Trees that weather the storm get wet and their limbs blow in the wind. Many even get battered by the storms. Battered and tattered but not destroyed! The trees are shaken, but they are not (uprooted) moved!! Similarly, as we weather the storms of life we are affected by the storms and we may be shaken by the storms, but we are not destroyed by them. Our trust and faith in the Lord is not uprooted and destroyed! The Lord's truth is our shield and buckler. Psalm 91:4. God is our refuge during troubling times. Psalm 46:1.

We must solely rely upon the Lord at all times. We have to (daily) resist the tendency and temptation to lean upon our own understanding. Sometimes we can think and think about our trouble or pain and ponder it in our hearts and before we know it defeat, fear, depression began to settle in. Our own understanding is finite. It is very limited. God on the other hand, knows all things because he is omniscient. He has all the answers to our why's, when's and how's. We must simply trust him. We must trust Him to keep us while we are in the storm. We must trust Him to protect us while the fiery tests are raging all around us. We must trust Him even when it seems as if he has left or forsaken us. We sometimes have to remind ourselves that the Lord has promised to never leave us or forsake us!! Hebrews 13:5b. Furthermore, God has the final authority over our lives. It is very refreshing to know that the doctors don't have the final authority, the reports of men/women don't have the final authority . . . God and God alone has the final authority!

I can remember a time when my husband and I suffered a very tragic situation, the loss of our unborn baby. We were so excited to be pregnant and the unexpected happened. The Lord immediately spoke to our hearts to trust Him, and to lean not to our own understanding. He said for us to acknowledge Him and he would direct our paths. After this tragic incident occurred I reported back to work within a couple of days. Some of my co-workers were devastated by the news of what had happened. Many were shocked about me returning to work so soon. Others were equally shocked that I came in with a smile and I comforted those that grieved for me and with me. How was I able to do this? It was not in my own strength, but in the strength of the Lord. Did the tragedy affect me? Yes it did. My heart was broken, but I quickly gave the broken pieces to the Lord. I refused to try to figure out the whys and I purposefully focused on God and His love and power. Why? Because, even in our most heart breaking situations, and times of tragedy, God is STILL faithful. He is still ruling and reigning. He has not left or forsaken us. He is forever faithful!

It is also very important to note another definition of trust. Trust also means to surrender complete control and care. You can, for example, trust someone with the care of your child, or with the responsibility of your money. Likewise, you can trust the Lord with your heart and life, your family, your finances, etc. When one trusts the Lord with their whole heart, they are literally surrendering complete control and authority of their hearts, minds and lives to the Lord. This surrender can not take place without total trust in God. He is the one that created us. He knows how much we can bear. He knows our hearts better than we do. He can and will take care of us! As I mentioned before, the Bible tells us to "cast all of our cares upon the Lord because he cares for us." 1 Peter 5: 7. The word cast means to throw upon, to entrust with. Our cares are those people, places, situations and things that weigh heavy on our hearts. Simply put, cares are our personal concerns. God is concerned about us. He is concerned about our cares and concerns!

As we acknowledge God as God . . . all powerful and all knowing, he will begin to direct our paths. He will lead and guide us through every dark and difficult time. As I mentioned earlier, when we come to God (in prayer) we must first believe that He is God and that he is a rewarder to those that diligently seek Him. Hebrews 11:6. Believing that God is indeed GOD means that we know without a shadow of a doubt, that God is the one in power and authority!

CHAPTER 8

Tears

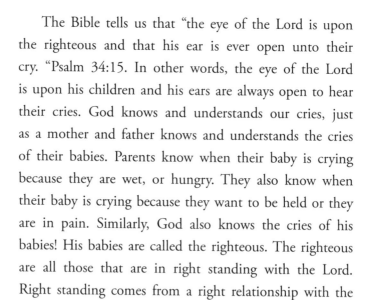

The Bible tells us that "the eye of the Lord is upon the righteous and that his ear is ever open unto their cry. "Psalm 34:15. In other words, the eye of the Lord is upon his children and his ears are always open to hear their cries. God knows and understands our cries, just as a mother and father knows and understands the cries of their babies. Parents know when their baby is crying because they are wet, or hungry. They also know when their baby is crying because they want to be held or they are in pain. Similarly, God also knows the cries of his babies! His babies are called the righteous. The righteous are all those that are in right standing with the Lord. Right standing comes from a right relationship with the

Lord. The Bible states: "little children, let no man deceive you: he that doeth righteousness is righteous, even as he is righteous." 1 John 3: 7. A right relationship with Lord can only be established by a sincere and heartfelt acceptance of the atoning blood sacrifice for one's sins. This sacrifice was lovingly given to us by Jesus Christ. The only thing that can wash away the sins of mankind, which includes your sin and mine, is the precious, sin free blood of Jesus Christ. Jesus sacrificed his life so that we could have eternal life and freedom from the bondages of sin! Accepting this sacrifice means acknowledging that God is God (acknowledge that God is indeed sovereign) and that His only begotten son is Jesus. It also means acknowledging that you are a sinner (all have sinned and fallen short of the glory of God, Romans 3:23 . . . . and we were born into sin and shaped in iniquity) and that you need a savior. The next step is to repent—which means you ask the Lord Jesus to forgive you of your sins. Repent also means to turn away from your sins. Thus, you turn away from your sin and you turn toward the Lord. God knows that there some areas that we all struggle with . . . but if we have a sincere and honest heart toward Him and want to be more like Him each and everyday . . . God will give us grace and he will help us. We must resist all temptation to justify or make excuses for our sin or areas of weaknesses. Ask Him to wash you from every sin. Ask the Lord Jesus to live in your heart today. Ask Him to be your Lord (ruler) and Savior (deliverer and rescuer) today!

"The eye of the Lord is upon the righteous . . . ." Psalm 34:15. When I think about the eye of the Lord being upon me I feel such comfort, strength and peace. I can literally feel the love of God surrounding me and engulfing me. In fact, I am reminded of how mindful the Lord is about his people. He cares so very much for us and about us. The Bible tells us that the very hairs on our head are numbered. Matthew 10:30. Wow! Please take a moment and think about your hair. Every day your hair healthily sheds strands. The Lord is very mindful of us. He keeps a count of the number of hairs on our head!! With the daily natural shedding process, the Lord is so very concerned about us—he keeps daily and accurate counts of the number of hair strands on each one of our heads! The Bible also tells us that God keeps track of our comings and our goings. Psalm 37:23. Our footsteps are even accounted for!

I can remember many times of undergoing trouble, heartache and pain. During these difficult times I would cry, weep and sob unto the Lord. The devil would tell me that Lord didn't care and he was not concerned about my tears. Not So! How far from the truth! The Bible says that God collects our tears in a bottle. Psalm 56:8 Our tears are just that precious to the Lord! He collects our tears in a bottle! I can envision a "tear room" in heaven. In this room are rows and rows of shelves filled with bottles that contain the many tears of God's people. I imagine that some bottles are half full and others are nearly full. I also imagine that each bottle is labeled with the name of a born again believer. Each bottle reflects the life of a tried, tested and overcoming believer!

The Lord is so concerned about His people! This concern is evidenced by the following: God's eyes are upon us and his ears are open to our cries. Psalm 34:15. God accounts for the numbers of hairs on our heads and the very footsteps that we take! Last, but not least, just as a jeweler collects fine jewelry, God collects the tears of His people! Hallelujah!!

As I began to think about the tears that God's people cry, the Lord quickened me to study a little more. Naturally speaking, there are 3 types of tears that people can cry. The first type of tear is called the basal tear. The Basal tear is the natural wetness of the eye. This wetness or moisture keeps the eye protected from dust particles. The second type of tear is called the reflex tear. This tear occurs when your eyes are exposed to an irritant such as a freshly cut onion. It also occurs when you eat something that is very hot and spicy. The last type of tear is connected to the emotions and the heart. It is called the weeping and sobbing tear. These tears occur when a person experiences strong negative or strong positive heartfelt emotions. The amazing thing about these tears is their physical make-up is very different from the prior mentioned tears. The weeping tear contains more protein based hormones.

It also contains a stress hormone which is a natural pain killer. The Lord is so amazing! He has a purpose and a special design to our tears! When one cries because of a painful situation or circumstance, for example, their very tears contain a healing mechanism that heals and relieves the person's pain. That is why one feels better after they have had a "good" cry.

CHAPTER 9

Hope for the future

Several years ago I went to a local department store. As I walked in I noticed a lady, an elderly lady, a little girl about 5 years old and a young man about ten years old. They appeared to be a family. The lady was a petite lady and the elderly lady was also small. The five year old was average sized and the ten year old boy was tall and very stocky. I noticed this family as I shopped. A few minutes passed and suddenly I heard a loud outburst. As I looked around to find out the source and cause of the loud noise I was very surprised to see the ten year old boy screaming and pulling the petite lady and the elderly lady. The ladies were sweating as they tried to calm him down. The young man appeared to be very strong as the 2 women sort of dangled by his hands and arms. The other shoppers and store employees began to gather around and stare as the 2 small women struggled to calm the ten year old. Some of the onlookers even began to make rude comments about the situation. Although I did not fully understand what was going on, my heart went out to this family and I immediately began to pray for them. As I prayed, the Lord spoke to my heart. He said, "that child has autism." At this time, I had a very limited understanding about autism. Emmanuel had not yet been born. I would of never imagined that I would one day face similar challenges. The Lord did know however. And it seems as if the Lord has used many experiences, tests and trials to prepare me and my husband to raise our son. In fact, I am awed, humbled and thankful for God and His divine providence!

I remember my first few years of teaching in a public school. I had a principal that had very strong beliefs about educating all children (typically and non-typically developing) and about having a fully included school. Several teachers expressed anxiety and resistance to the idea of full inclusion. I decided to pray about this situation. I prayed for the staff and for the school principal. I also prayed a special yet simple prayer for my own classroom. As I remember the prayer went like this:" Dear Lord, please select each and every student that will be placed in my classroom. Give me the grace to reach each and every student, in Jesus Name. Amen."

Well about a week after praying that prayer, the principal knocked on my classroom door. She had a look of great concern on her face. She said: "Mrs. Williams, will you please take _____ in your classroom? (I will call this student Michelle to protect her privacy and identity). The principal went on to say: "I truly believe that she will prosper in your classroom." As I got ready to give the principal an answer, the Lord reminded me of the prayer that I had prayed. I quickly answered the principal: "Yes, I will take her!" As I gave this answer, I could feel my knees shaking and my heart beating real fast. The principal looked relieved and said, "Great! I will bring her to your classroom tomorrow." "Michelle" was a 5 year old that was the height and weight of an 8 year old! She was a chubby yet beautiful child. I had witnessed her and her behavior many times as she seemed to spend more time walking the halls with her one on one assistant than in her classroom. She had a smile that would light up a room, and mindset of her own. She had limited verbal language, but she was well able to communicate her wants, likes and dislikes. She wore a helmet because she would bang her head when she was upset and also for protection as she was prone to have seizures.

I was concerned about "Michelle" and I wanted her to do well in my class. I wanted her to "fit in" with my typically developing students. I took my cares and concerns to the Lord. He told us to "cast all of our cares upon him, because he cares for us." 1 Peter 5:7. I asked the Lord to remove her helmet and to keep her safe. The helmet seemed to mark her as a special or different. I wanted her comfortably blend in with the rest of my students.

The next day the principal brought "Michelle" to my classroom. I met her at the door and I shook Michelle's hand and said welcome to your new classroom! Michelle smiled and stepped over the threshold of my classroom door. She immediately stopped and put both of her hands on her helmet. She said: "Helmet off! Helmet off!" I smiled, because I knew that the Lord had heard and answered my prayer. The principal took her helmet off and said "Well, we must respect her wishes!"

"Michelle" remained in my classroom for one school year. She never had a tantrum and she never banged her head. In fact, she did have several seizures, but God always warned me, or my assistant teacher, or the one on one assistant that a seizure was coming. God would grace us with a warning and we would tell "Michelle" to lie down—while we called the school office for help.

"Michelle" did prosper in my classroom. Glory to God! She no longer spent more time in the hallway than in the classroom. She greeted me each day with a smile and a hug. One day she said: "teacher I love you."

I am so very thankful for all of my teaching experiences. I believe that the Lord used these experiences to prepare me for the time that I would later give birth to our son Emmanuel. God knew that I would one day have a child that would have special needs. God prepared my heart a long time ago for the journey that my husband and I are traveling now. A journey of testing and trial. A journey of faith, hope and victory!

Several years later I gave birth to our son Emmanuel. He was diagnosed with autism at the age of 4 years old. About a year or so after our son was diagnosed with autism, my husband and I decided to get connected with the autism community in our city and state. We attended various support group meetings, walkathons, community events, etc. It was both bitter and sweet to meet so many different families whose lives were touched by autism. The common denominator was autism and the shared emotion was hurt and pain. As I looked upon the countenance of each person and or family the Lord allowed me to see their inner hurt and pain. Many have spoken about their hurts, about their dashed dreams, daily struggles, disappointments, etc. Many have suffered in silence. Out of all the people we have met along the way, out of all the speeches and talks that we have listened to about autism, the missing factor has often been hope. Faith deals with the present and hope refers to the future.

The Bible tells us: "For we are saved by hope: but hope that is seen is not hope: for what a man seeth, why doth he yet hope for? But if we hope for that we see not, then do we with patience wait for it." Romans 8:24-25. This scripture tells us that we are saved by hope. In other words, we are rescued, delivered, freed, healed, redeemed by our relentless hope in God. We hope for the things that we do not currently have. Hope consists of the cries and desires of our hearts. Hope also consists of the answers to the prayers that we have voiced and the ones that we have not. Our hopes are also the dreams that we hold near and dear. They include the promises that God has given us in the Bible. As we continually put our hope and faith in the Lord, the prior mentioned scripture reminds us we are to patiently wait for the thing(s) that we are hopping for. The word patient means to make a determination to persist, in spite of trouble, problems or difficulty. We are to eagerly wait for what we are hoping for.

. The Bible tells us that Abraham maintained his hope in God. God had made him a promise that he would be the father of many nations, and the heir of the world. Abraham persisted in his hope and he believed what God had spoken to him. God still speaks to His people! He speaks in numerous ways—through His Holy Bible, through his preachers and teachers, in a still small voice, through the voice of a stranger, etc. Many years passed since the time in which God had made the promise to Abraham. During this time, Abraham and his wife remained childless. The Bible tells us: "Who (Abraham) against hope believed in hope, that he might become the father of many nations, according to that which was spoken, SO SHALL THY SEED BE." Romans 4: 18. Abraham and his wife waited 25 years for the manifestation of God's promise. Their bodies grew old and they were well beyond child bearing age. But Abraham maintained His hope in the Lord. The Bible states that Abraham was not weak in faith, Romans 4: 19, and thus, he did not even consider how at age 100 his own body was dead (as far as reproduction was concerned) neither did he consider the deadness of his wife Sarah's womb.

The Bible clearly states: "He (Abraham) staggered not at the promise of God through unbelief: but was strong in faith, giving Glory to God; and being fully persuaded that, what he had promised, he was also able to perform." Romans 4:20-21.

Are you fully persuaded about the promises of God? EVERY biblical promise is for God's children! Please remember our life and times are in the hand of the Lord. (Psalm 31:14-15) We are to place our hope, trust and faith solely in Him. "Be of good courage, and he (the Lord) shall strengthen your heart, all ye that hope in the Lord." Psalm 31:24.

Chapter 10

When God? When . . . ?

As you are standing in faith and maintaining your hope, please know that we are on the Lord's time clock. His concept of time is quite different from ours. "But, beloved, be not ignorant of this one thing, that one day is with the Lord as a thousand years, and a thousand years as one day. The Lord is not slack concerning his promise, as some men count slackness; but is longsuffering to us-ward, not willing that any should perish, but that all should come to repentance." II Peter 3: 8-9.

Be encouraged as you are standing and waiting on the full manifestation of God's promises. Make a steadfast decision to continue to walk in faith and hope even when the timing of the Lord seems prolonged. We now live in the drive-thru and microwave generation. We want things to happen quick, fast and in a hurry!! Some blessings, breakthroughs and answers to prayer will occur in an immediate fashion. While other breakthroughs and answers to prayer will occur as we continue to wholeheartedly serve God and walk in faith. There is a blessing in the waiting. Can you imagine giving a child everything they ever wanted at the exact time of their desire and request? That child would never learn patience, endurance, perseverance, the value of labor and hard work, etc. As we wait on the Lord to manifest his promises and answer our prayers, the Lord builds character in us. He builds endurance. He draws us closer to Him. Yes, there are many blessings in the wait! Every test and trial that we endure has a divine purpose. The Lord wants us to grow better and not bitter. He wants us to grow stronger in our faith. He wants us to know and understand his divine character, nature and awesome attributes. You can never have a testimony without first having a test! God has called us, and paved the way for us to overcome EVERY test!! "And they overcame him (Satan and his tricks and schemes) by the blood of the Lamb (Jesus), and by the word of their testimony; and they loved not their lives unto the death." Revelation 12:11.

So we overcome every adversity, every challenge, every hardship, every pain by the shed blood of Jesus. Jesus' blood was shed for the remission of our sins, for our healing, for our peace, and for our victory in every

CHAPTER 11

If God is GOD then why is there sickness & disease?

———◆———

If God is GOD then why is there sickness and disease? Lord why did my child have to suffer with this sickness? Why was my child afflicted with this disability? Why did my relative die of cancer? These are the heartfelt, yet heart wrenching questions that are often pondered in the hearts and minds of many. Although I am not God, I will use the scriptures to provide a response. I pray that in some way, the Lord will use me to bring some degree of understanding and even a glimmer of God's love, peace and hope.

Romans 5:12 reads: "Wherefore, as by one man sin entered into the world, and death by sin: and so death passed upon all men, for that we all have sinned." It all began in the book of Genesis. In the book of Genesis, God gave Adam a clear command: "And the Lord God commanded the man (Adam), saying, Of every tree of the garden thou mayest freely eat: but of the tree of the knowledge of good and evil, thou shalt not eat it: for in the day that thou shalt eatest thereof thou shalt surely die." Genesis 2: 16-17. Adam disobeyed God's command. He ate from the tree of the knowledge of good and evil. Disobedience is sin. Sin is all unrighteousness and when one disobeys God it is indeed sin. Whether one chooses to sin or "falls" into sin, the effects of sin are long reaching, long ranging and long lasting. The effects of sin are long reaching because many others are directly affected by the sin choices of one individual. The effects of sin are long ranging because various areas of life and living are directly affected by the sin of one individual. And lastly, the effects of sin are long lasting . . . . lasting for many generations. Thus, when Adam sinned, sin entered and infiltrated the world and all future generations.

The sin that Adam and Eve committed caused death—both a spiritual and physical death. The spiritual death represents a broken and severed relationship between man and God. The severed relationship between man and God ultimately leads to an eternal death. Eternal death literally means dying and being tormented forever in the lake of fire (Revelations 20:10, 14). Lastly, there is the physical death. This is a death that every person will experience because of Adam's fall. This death represents a separation of the body from the spirit and soul. When the body physically dies, the spirit and soul leaves the body and will reside for eternity, either in heaven or hell.

Because of Adam's fall—we are all born into a world of sin and shaped in iniquity. Moreover, we are all born with a sin nature. The Scripture tells us: "all have sinned and fall short of the glory of God." Romans 3:23. Thus, we are not born into right relationship or in a right standing/position with God. We are born into a severed relationship and a wrong standing position with the Lord. The good news is we can receive righteousness or a right standing with God through faith in Jesus Christ. Faith in Jesus means believing in and trusting in Him. It means asking him to forgive you of your sins. It also means asking him to live in your heart. It means accepting Jesus as your Lord (ruler) and Savior.

Romans 3:22-25 says: "Even the righteousness of God which is by faith of Jesus Christ unto all and upon all them that believe: for there is no difference: For all have sinned, and come short of the glory of God. Being justified freely by his grace through the redemption that is in Christ Jesus: Whom God hath set forth to be a propitiation through faith in his blood, to declare his righteousness for the remission of sins that are past, through the forbearance of God . . ."

Thus, the sin committed by Adam and Eve opened the doorway to sickness, disease, hardships, etc., for the entire world. However, these doorways can be closed by the faith—filled, scripture based prayers of God's people. Psalm 103: 1-4. "Bless the Lord, O my soul: and all that is within me, bless his holy name. Bless the Lord, O my soul, and forget not all his benefits: Who forgiveth all thine iniquities; who healeth all thy diseases; [4] Who redeemeth thy life from destruction; who crowneth thee with loving kindness and tender mercies . . ."

One of the benefits of having a right relationship with God is forgiveness for all sins and healing from all diseases. The key is ALL. ALL sins includes: what man deems as "big" sins, what man deems as "little" sins, hidden sins, outright sins, generational sins, sins of commission, sins of omission . . . . ALL sin!!! Glory to God!! I am rejoicing because when I asked the Lord to forgive my sins He did!!! He put them in a sea called Forgetfulness, never to be remembered again!!! Micah 7:19. Hallelujah!!

The other awesome benefit of salvation is healing. According the Psalm 103: 3 the Lord heals his people of ALL diseases! Diseases include EVERY ailment, disorder, malfunction, pain, and symptom in the body and mind. As born again believers, we must know our rights and privileges. Yes, the Lord has blessed his children with many promises. As children of God we must grasp the promises of God and fervently apply them to our lives daily. What you don't know CAN & WILL hurt you!!! For example, if you didn't know that the Lord heals all our sickness and disease, you might just accept sickness as your plight in life. WRONG! Sickness and disease are not from GOD. God promises to heal us from sickness and disease! When you know your rights, you cannot be tricked out of them!

Many times Christians have the faith to believe that God will heal them. But they are often lacking in the total application of this promise of healing. God has given us power and authority over the works of Satan. "And when he had called unto him his twelve disciples, he gave them **power** against unclean spirits, to cast them out, and to heal all manner of sickness and all manner of disease." Matthew 10:1. We are his modern day disciples! The word disciple simply means follower. We are followers of the Lord Jesus Christ. Thus, as Christ's followers we have DELEGATED POWER & AUTHORITY (from Heaven). We have the power to reject sickness and disease. We can reject it with our words and with our actions. In other words, our words must be words of victory and healing, even in the midst of adverse symptoms and negative doctor's reports. We must train our tongues to speak life . . . speak what the Bible says about our situation and circumstances. The scripture tell us that we have the power to speak life or death. Proverbs 18:21. We must choose to speak life. We have to make a daily concerted decision to agree with the Word of the Lord (the Bible) and to speak what it says concerning our situations and circumstances. "Death and life are in the power of the tongue: and they that love it shall eat the fruit thereof." Proverbs 18:21.

We must resist the (daily) temptation to complain, and the temptation to walk in the land of Lodebar. We must leave pity at the party and press forward by faith in victory!!!! If we complain . . . we will remain! We will remain in the troubling and adverse situation/circumstance! The children of Israel learned this incredible truth when they murmured and complained while traveling through the wilderness. This complaining caused an 11 days journey to last for 40 long years!!

I read an article once about a lady that had a child with severe autism and severe behavior disorders. The child's parents were overwhelmed and they often complained about their child's negative behaviors. In fact, complaining became a regular part of their lifestyle. Until one day, the mother recommitted her life to the Lord, and started applying the "speaking life" principle. Instead of talking negatively about her child, she made a daily, conscious decision to speak life over her child. She spoke healing scriptures over her child every day. She no longer talked about the child's autism and behavior. By faith, she said her child was healed. Then one day, the healing manifested!! This non-verbal child began to speak!! The child spoke clearly and in full sentences!! His behavior totally changed. He left the special school and attended a school for typically developing students. That child is now an adult with several college degrees!!The Lord's healing had fully manifested!!! God's Word . . . his scriptures are powerful and full of life!!

"For as the rain cometh down, and the snow from heaven, and returneth not thither, but watereth the earth, and maketh it bring forth and bud, that it may give seed to the sower, and bread to the eater: So shall my word be that goeth forth out of my mouth: it shall not return unto me void, but it shall accomplish that which I please, and it shall prosper in the thing whereto I sent it." Isaiah 55:10-11.

God's Word, the scriptures in the Bible NEVER return to Him void, which means empty and default. His WORD accomplishes what it is sent out to do. The key to this accomplishment is faith. If we continue to walk in faith and talk in faith then God's perfect will can and will be accomplished. His perfect will is that his children understand their rights, privileges and delegated spiritual authority . . . . and apply them, walk in them every day of their lives!!

Although sickness entered the world when Adam and Eve sinned, it is important to note that all sickness is not the result of sin. "And as Jesus passed by, he saw a man which was blind from his birth. And his disciples asked him, saying, Master, who did sin, this man, or his parents, that he was born blind? Jesus answered, Neither hath this man sinned, nor his parents: but that the works of God should be made manifest in him." John 9:1-3. God allowed this man to be born blind so that the Glory of God, the miraculous healing power of God may be manifested in the earth!

CHAPTER 12

Notable Conditions in the Bible: Mental, Physical & Emotional Conditions

---◆---

<u>*The Blood of Jesus Prevails Over EVERY Condition!!!</u>

<u>Blind</u> (cannot see) Matthew 12:22

<u>Death</u> (cannot hear) Matthew 12:22.

<u>Dumb</u> (cannot speak) Matthew 12:22.

<u>Lame/halt</u> (crippled, has difficulty walking) Matthew 11:15; 2 Samuel 4: 4; Acts 3:2-8.

<u>Maimed</u> (disfigured; the loss of a limb i.e., hand or foot or the inability to use a limb) Matthew 15:30.

<u>Palsy</u> (some or all muscles are paralyzed, also includes involuntary muscle movements) Mark 2: 2-12.

<u>Lunatick</u> (epilepsy, seizures) Mark 17:15, Matthew 4:24.

<u>"Grievously vexed with a devil"</u> (no description given) Matthew 15:22-28.

<u>"Man with an unclean spirit"</u>: (had great strength—chains could not bind him, Self injurious behavior—cut himself with stones, cried excessively, could not be "tamed", would not wear clothes, remained isolated in the mountains) Mark 5: 2-20.

<u>Leprosy</u>: (Known as an unclean disease. Causes lesions on skin and disfigurement of body parts) Leviticus 13: 44-46; Mark 1:40-42.

<u>Slow of Speech/Slow tongue</u> (stuttering) Exodus 4:10-16.

<u>Barren</u> (unable to conceive a child) Genesis 25:21: Luke 1:36; I Samuel 1:5-20.

<u>Fever</u> Mark 1:30-31.

<u>"Issue of blood"</u> (the blood flow would not stop—lased for 12 years): Luke 8: 43-48.

<u>Atrophy</u> (when the body deteriorates and wastes away) Job Chapter 16.

<u>Boils</u>: (painful skin infection) 2 King 20:7.

<u>Insanity</u> (lack of clear understanding): Daniel 4:33-34.

<u>Tumors</u>: (swelling in the skin, can be cancerous or non-cancerous) Deuteronomy 28:27.

<u>Scurvy</u>: (scaliness of the skin) Deuteronomy 28:27.

<u>Itch</u>: (a disorder of the skin that includes irritated skin) Deuteronomy 28:27.

CHAPTER 13

Recognize, Remember and Receive the Miracles

Sometimes people don't recognize miracles. Other times, people take miracles lightly and treat them as if they are just ordinary daily occurrences. I believe that we must take time to recognize miracles. Miracles are deeds and occurrences that only the Lord can authorize and perform. In my small time on earth, I have been blessed to see many miracles. I have seen the Lord shrink cancerous tumors that would not respond to expensive medications, chemotherapy or radiation. In fact, the golf ball sized tumor shrank (and completely dissipated) ONLY after prayer! I have also witnessed the Lord completely heal a mother from full blown AIDS and her newborn baby from HIV. Oh, the POWER of PRAYER!!! I also witnessed the Lord instantly give perfect speech to a non verbal teenager and instantly grow someone's leg that was shorter than the other. "But Jesus beheld them, and said unto them, With men this is impossible; but with God all things are possible." Matthew 19:26.

As we continue to walk the walk of faith and travel on this Christian journey we must take time to remember the miracles. Yes . . . we must remember the miracles! What miracles?? The miracles that are described in the Bible. The miracles that we have read about, heard about and or personally witnessed. Every time we recall the miracles that the Lord has performed we receive strength and we are empowered to overcome the devil. The Bible tells us: "And they overcame him (Satan) by the blood of the Lamb, and by the word of their testimony; and they loved not their lives unto the death." Revelation 12:11. The blood of the lamb is referring to the shed blood of Jesus Christ. The Blood of Jesus never loses its power. Thus, we overcome the devil by reflecting on the testimonies listed in the Bible, by our own testimonies and the testimonies of others.

We also overcome by accepting the Blood sacrifice of Jesus Christ. We overcome by remembering all that Jesus did for us when he laid down His life at Calvary Cross. We overcome by applying the Blood of Jesus (through words of prayer) over every situation and circumstance.

There is deliverance in the Blood of Jesus. There is healing in the Blood of Jesus. There is redemption in the Blood of Jesus! There is power, wonder working power in the Blood of Jesus!!

CHAPTER 14

Healing Scriptures

―――――――――◇―――――――――

This chapter is simply comprised of some of my favorite healing scriptures. Read them. Meditate (think deeply) about them. Commit them to your heart and mind. Include them in your prayers.

"Bless the Lord, O my soul: and all that is within me, bless his holy name. Bless the Lord, O my soul, and forget not all his benefits: Who forgiveth all thine iniquities; who healeth all thy diseases; Who redeemeth thy life from destruction; who crowneth thee with loving kindness and tender mercies; Who satisfieth thy mouth with good things; so that thy youth is renewed like the eagle's." Psalm 103:1-5.

"Beloved, I wish above all things that thou mayest prosper and be in health, even as thy soul prospereth." 3 John 1:2.

"But he was wounded for our transgressions, he was bruised for our iniquities: the chastisement of our peace was upon him; and with his stripes we are healed." Isaiah 53:5.

"Then was brought unto him one possessed with a devil, blind, and dumb: and he healed him, insomuch that the blind and dumb both spake and saw." Matthew 12:22.

"And great multitudes came unto him, having with them those that were lame, blind, dumb, maimed, and many others, and cast them down at Jesus' feet; and he healed them: Insomuch that the multitude wondered, when they saw the dumb to speak, the maimed to be whole, the lame to walk, and the blind to see: and they glorified the God of Israel." Matthew 15: 30-31.

"And they that were vexed with unclean spirits: and they were healed. And the whole multitude sought to touch him: for there went virtue out of him, and healed them all." Luke 6: 18-19.

"And when he had called unto him his twelve disciples, he gave them power against unclean spirits, to cast them out, and to heal all manner of sickness and all manner of disease." Matthew 10:1.

"How God anointed Jesus of Nazareth with the Holy Ghost and with power: who went about doing good, and healing all that were oppressed of the devil; for God was with him." Acts 10:38.

"I shall not die, but live, and declare the works of the Lord." Psalm 118:17.

"Then they cry unto the Lord in their trouble, and he delivered them out of their distresses." Psalm 107:6.

He sent his word, and healed them, and delivered them from their destructions." Psalm 107:19-20.

"And Jesus said unto the centurion, Go thy way; and as thou hast believed, so be it done unto thee. And his servant was healed in the selfsame hour." Matthew 8:13.

"And when Jesus was come into Peter's house, he saw his wife's mother laid, and sick of a fever. And he touched her hand, and the fever left her: and she arose, and ministered unto them." Matthew 8:14-15.

"My son, attend to my words; incline thine ear unto my sayings. Let them not depart from thine eyes; keep them in the midst of thine heart. For they are life unto those that find them, and health to all their flesh." Proverbs 4:20-22.

"Is any among you afflicted (suffering)? let him pray. Is any merry? Let him sing psalms. Is any sick among you? Let him call for the elders of the church; and let them pray over him, anointing him with oil in the name of the Lord: And the prayer of faith shall save the sick, and the Lord shall raise him up; and if he has committed sins, they shall be forgiven him. Confess your faults one to another, and pray one for another, that ye may be healed. "The effectual fervent prayer of a righteous man availeth much." James: 5:13-16.

"And they bring unto him one that was deaf, and had an impediment in his speech; and they beseech him to put his hand upon him. And he took him aside from the multitude, and put his fingers into his ears, and he spit, and touched his tongue; And looking up to heaven, he sighed, and saith unto him, Ephphatha, that is, Be opened. And straightway his ears were opened, and the string of his tongue was loosed, and he spake plain." Mark 7:32-35.

"The blind receive their sight, and the lame walk, the lepers are cleansed, and the deaf hear, the dead are raised up, and the poor have the gospel preached to them." Matthew 11:5.

"Now when the sun was setting, all they that had any sick with divers diseases brought them unto him (Jesus); and he laid his hands on every one of them, and healed them." Luke 4:40.

"And Jesus went forth, and saw a great multitude, and was moved with compassion toward them, and he healed their sick." Matthew 14:14.

"And Jesus went about all Galilee, teaching in their synagogues, and preaching the gospel of the kingdom, and healing all manner of sickness and all manner of disease among the people." Matthew 4:23.

"And in that same hour he cured many of their infirmities and plagues, and of evil spirits; and unto many that were blind he gave sight." Luke 7:21.

"So shall my word be that goeth forth out of my mouth: it shall not return unto me void, but it shall accomplish that which I please, and it shall prosper in the thing whereto I sent it." Isaiah 55:11.

"Jesus Christ the same yesterday, and today, and forever." Hebrews 13:8.

CHAPTER 15

Prayers

"The effectual fervent prayer of a righteous man availeth much."

James 5:16b

Prayer for Salvation

Father I come to you, right now in the name of Jesus. I ask that you have your perfect will and way in my heart, life and soul. Wash me and cleanse me. Make me whole. Forgive me for every sin that I have committed. I repent Lord. I know that Jesus died for me and I now accept him as my Lord and savior. Lord means ruler. So I now allow Jesus to rule over my life. Savior means rescuer . . .

so I surrender and submit my life to Jesus. Thank you for saving me. In Jesus Name I pray!

Prayer for the Child with Special Needs

Father, I thank you that_____ is fearfully and wonderfully made. I thank you that you have a special plan and purpose for _____. I ask that you touch and raise up_____. I decree and declare healing over_____. According to Isaiah 53:5 _____ is healed by the stripes that Jesus received on His back at Calvary Cross. Quicken his or her mind. Restore all that has been stolen: restore perfect mental health. Restore perfect social-emotional health. Restore perfect physical health. Restore his/her speech and cognitive functioning, in Jesus name. Transform his/her behavior. Cause him/her to walk in peace and in obedience to authority, in Jesus name. Regulate every system and organ in their body. Make him/her whole, in Jesus Name! Cause him/her to defy every negative report, and statistic in Jesus name!!

Prayer for the Parents of a Child with Special Needs

Father, in the name of Jesus, touch every parent of a special needs child/adult. We cover them with the precious blood of Jesus Christ. Give them supernatural strength as they care for their child/ children, in Jesus name! Encourage them as they advocate for their child. Encourage them as they tend to their daily affairs. Give them wisdom and understanding as it concerns their child with special needs. Provide them with a support system that willingly and generously gives assistance, encouragement and respite in Jesus name. Increase their faith in you. Lord, help them to walk by faith and not by sight. Give them the courage and power to rise above challenging situations and circumstances, In Jesus name!!

A Special Prayer for Single Parents

Father, in the mighty name of Jesus, give an extra dose of strength and encouragement to all of the single parents that are raising a child/children with autism. Make their realm of support large. Meet and exceed their every need. Increase their faith and trust in you each and every day. In Jesus Name we pray, Amen!!

Prayer for Marriages that have an Autism Connection

Father in the name of Jesus, touch every marriage that includes a child with autism. Strengthen each marital union. We take authority over Satan and bind up every evil tactic, plan and scheme in Jesus name. We bind up stress, strain, pain and anguish in Jesus name. We ask that the Lord knit the married couples so tightly together that not even a straight pin would be able to get in and separate them. Help them to make time for one another and to build their marriage, in Jesus Name.

Prayer for the Siblings of Children With Special needs

Father, touch every sibling of a special needs child, in Jesus Name. We cover them with the precious blood of Jesus. Give them clear understanding as it relates to their sibling with special needs. Lavish them with love, affection and attention. Erase away any feelings of stress, worry, or neglect that they may have concerning their family. Give them a support network that supports and encourages them. Strengthen them and encourage them day by day. Make a way for them to have one on one time with their parents. Amen.

Prayer for Special Educators & Therapists

Father, in the name of Jesus, I ask that you touch each special educator and therapist of special children. Give them wisdom, insight, understanding, patience, compassion, stamina and effective strategies as they work with children/ adults with special needs. Bless them with an awesome support network as they seek to help children and or adults with special needs. Give them a heart filled with compassion and wisdom. Help them to reach every student that they encounter, in Jesus Name.

Prayers for Administrators of Schools With Special Needs Students

Lord, I ask that you lead and guide every administrator in Jesus Name. Strengthen them. Encourage them. Help them to make mindful and righteous decisions concerning students with special needs and their families. Give them an understanding heart and a heart of compassion. Help them to be awesome leaders over their school staff. Give them school staffs that are willing to work in a collaborative fashion, in Jesus Name. Meet and exceed the needs of their schools in Jesus name!

Prayer for School Bus Drivers (that transport children with special needs) and Bus Monitors

Father, in the name of Jesus, touch every school bus driver and bus monitor. Help them to greet each and every student with a smile and a hello. Give them safe travel every day as they transport students/ adults with special needs. Give them an understanding and compassion for each student. Give them wisdom as they encounter each child. We pray for safe travel, in Jesus Name.

A Prayer for College Professors that Teach Special Education Courses

Lord, touch each college professor. Give them a heartfelt desire to teach content and "soft skills." Soft skills include how to effectively talk to and interact with special students as well as with their parents and families. Soft skills also include having a heart of compassion with a willingness to understand the needs of each child and the daily challenges that parents and families encounter.

Lord, give each professor a desire to become an advocate for children with special needs. Encourage each professor to pass that love and advocacy on to their college students (pre-service special educators), in Jesus Name.

Chapter 16

The Final Word

Years ago, I took a college class entitled Survey of Exceptional Children. This class required the use of one textbook. The title of the textbook was <u>Exceptional Children: An Introduction to Special Education</u>, written by William L. Heward, Fifth Edition. This text book was written in 1996. On page 489, it states "it is estimated that autism occurs in approximately 5 out of every 10,000 children."

Today, less than 20 years later, the number of children diagnosed with autism is troubling and stifling! According to Autism Speaks and the Center for Disease Control, 1 in 88 children will be diagnosed with autism and 1 in

54 boys will be diagnosed with autism. The numbers are escalating each and every year.

Autism crosses racial lines, ethnicity lines, and class lines. It is not discriminatory. It is my heartfelt prayer that the causes of Autism be uncovered as well as a cure discovered.

The final word, however is not the current statistics. It is not what we see and hear. The final word is our word. The final word is what comes out of our mouths each and every day. We have power to speak death and life. We must choose to speak life. We must make a determination in our hearts to speak life. The Word of God is life. Thus, we must speak what the Word of God says. What we see, what we feel and what we hear is often opposite of the Word of God. We must resist the temptation to speak those words!! Jesus used his words to curse a fig tree that was not bearing fruit. Mark 11:13, 20. The tree withered up and died the very next day. I sometimes shudder when I think about this. Our words that line up with the Word of God are life giving words . . . . Words that speak blessing. But our idle words are often contrary to the Word of God and therefore are death-giving words. In actuality they are words that speak curses. We must make a daily determination to speak the Words of life over our children, situations and circumstances!!!

Let's look a little closer at the power of our words: "Jesus answered and said unto them, Verily I say unto you, If ye have faith, and doubt not, ye shall not only do this which is done to the fig tree, but also if ye shall say unto this mountain, Be thou removed, and be thou cast into the sea; it shall be done. And all things, whatsoever ye shall ask in prayer, believing, ye shall receive." Matthew 21:21-22. Jesus said: "Ye shall SAY to this mountain . . . .." At some point we all encounter mountains. Mountains represent gigantic-sized tests, trials, tribulations. It seems like the more we focus on the mountains . . . the bigger they become! Compared to God, and his infinite power, the mountains and the giants are the size of a tiny insect!!! Glory to God!!!

Let's take a closer look at the mountains. Naturally speaking, mountains are humongous rocks. According to Jeremiah 23: 29, "Is not my word like as a fire? saith the Lord; and like a hammer that breaketh the rock in pieces?" Fire cleanses and purifies, Thus, God's Word cleanses us and purifies us. However, when we stand in faith in the midst of adverse situations and circumstances and we apply the Word of God . . . something happens! The applied Word of God, Holy Scriptures, Bible verses, acts as a hammer to break the rock into pieces. Mountains are gigantic sized rocks! So as we consistently and persistently apply the Word of God, we are applying pressure—earth shattering pressure to the mountain!! It is important to note, however, that initially one may not see a physical change in the mountain. When a person takes a hammer and hammers a rock, the rock begins to crack from the inside out. In other words, the initial cracks begin on the inside of the rock and are not visible on the outside of the rock. Thus, one must remain faithful and steadfast in the business of hammering! Refuse to be shaken or moved by how things look on the outside!! For the Christian, hammering is the daily practice of applying the Word of God, and standing on the promises of God! It is the faithful practice of speaking what the Word of God says over everyday situations and circumstances.

As I close, I strongly encourage you to remain prayerful. Walk in total anticipation and expectation for the Lord's deliverance. I leave you with a Final Word . . . my son's favorite scripture that he memorized at the age of 3.

> **"But Jesus beheld them, and said unto them, With men this is impossible; but with God all things are possible."**
>
> **Matthew 19:26.**

References

Autism Speaks. (n.d.). *What is autism?*. Retrieved from http://www.autismspeaks.org/what-autism

Heward, William L., (Ed). (1996.). *Exceptional children: an introduction to special education* (5th ed.). Upper Saddle River, NJ: Prentiss Hall Press.

The Holy Bible, King James Version